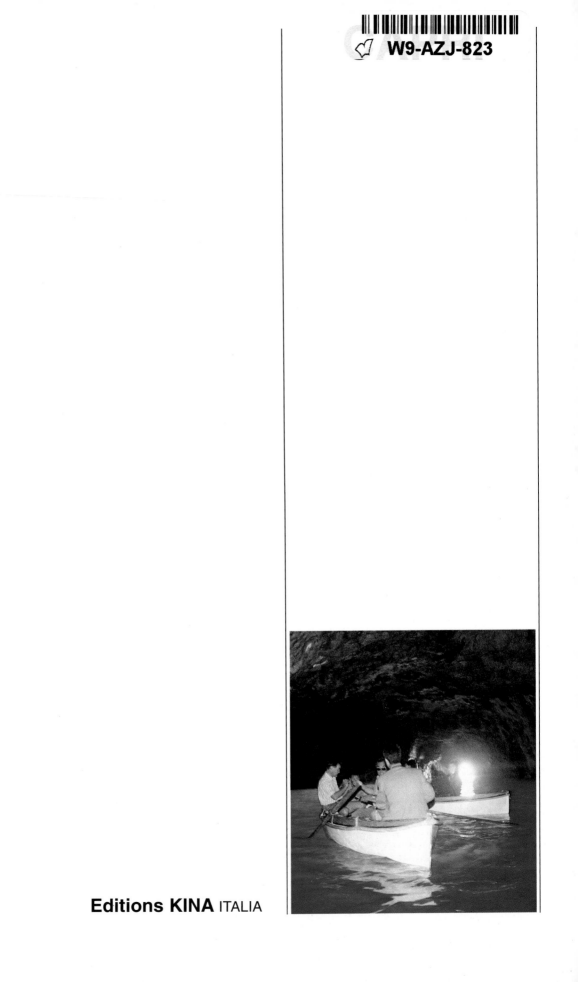

CAPRI

W9-AZJ-823

Editions KINA ITALIA

INDEX

"*Cauros*" (i.e. wild boar, for its characteristic shape) to the ancient Greek colonists, "*Capraea*" and "*Insula Sirenussae*" (i.e. bitter, rocky island and mermaids' island) to the Latins, "*Antheomoessa*" (i.e. Land in flower) to Homer, "*Apragopolis*" (i.e. land of sweet idleness) to Emperor Augustus: these names and nicknames, conjuring up bitterness and sweetness at the same time, assigned to the island of Capri over the centuries are probably enough to describe the various aspects of this land of matchless beauty and enchantment.

The island, which is quite small (its perimeter is no longer than 17 km), is almost completely formed by limestone rock which, during the course of the millenniums, the elements and geological movements have modelled into mountainous reliefs (the highest peak, Monte Solaro, reaches an altitude of 589 m); they drop more gently down into a series of rolling hills and two large plateaus divided at the neck of the island, between Marina Grande and Marina Piccola, which in turn drop down to the sea often in the form of steep, jagged cliffs indented in small creeks, caves and ravines, or projecting in mini peninsulas and headlands that offer unforgettable panoramas, or even adorned with rocks or gigantic masses that emerge majestically from the water. On this land, the vegetation has grown in line with the climate, always mild and quite dry, colouring the rock green with woods and spontaneous vegetation, low and thick, or with the lively colours of its numerous flowers, colours which have been enriched over the course of the centuries with those of grapes, olive trees and citrus fruit plantations cultivated by man in the more fertile areas. A perfect natural environment (which is today actively protected) for numerous animal species, living both on the land and in the water, common or rare like the *Podarcis sicula coerulea*, the famous blue lizard that only lives on one of the island's Faraglioni rocks. Capri, the "paradise of *idleness*", to call it as Emperor Augustus did, i.e. away from the pressures of daily working life, to be dedicated to the discovery of nature and the many historical and artistic beauties of the island: the deep sea, the matchless panoramas, the picturesque villages, the ruins of ancient Roman villas, the Charterhouse and the churches, the castles, palaces, the countless private villas, the towers, the caves... These are probably the mermaids that figure in the legends which, with their melodious and irresistible charm attracted onto the island not only two emperors but also a large number of painters, writers, musicians, scholars and artists who found inspiration for their works or simply wished to pay homage to Capri, "Reina de roca, en tu vestido de amaranto y azucena", (Queen of Rock, in your cockscomb and white lily robe), as Pablo Naruda wrote.

MARE

P. dell' Arcera
Grotta Azzurra
Gr.ta Guarracini
P. di Gràdola
la Selva
P. Sbruffo
P. Trasete
Gr.ta dei Mandri
Bagno di T.

P. di Vetereto
Torre Damecuta
33
30
120
Linaro Artimo
222
V.la Debalac
267
24
Palazzo a M.
153 151
130
153
223
C.de Tommaso
55

P. del Miglio
Osservatorio Astrofisico
167
221
Capodimonte
269
Pàstena
S. Antonio
246
Cast.o Barbarossa
Mad.na della Grotta
40
159
Strada di
175
248
il Pozzo
Via G. Orlandi
286

P. Capocchia
160
112
79
49
Via Lo Pozzo
275
Anacapri
282
464
di Ana

Gr.ta Iannarella
180
196
232
Boffe
Via Boffe
286
Caposcuro
340

Cala Lupinaro
Cala del Rio
130
156
225
M.o a vento
Via Tuoro
Via Monticello
Pagliaro
258
Paradiso
272
Catena
286
491
M. Cappello
514
M. S. Mari
491

24
110
Fràito
175
Caprile
250
268
290
Caruso

P. Campetiello
39
37
Materita
189
301
451
523
Osserv.o Solare
503
S. M. Cet
476

il Latino
57
113
il Pino
M. Solaro
589
486
Gr.ta dell' Arco

Cala di mezzo
187
79
196
Fortino di Bruto
360
192

P. del Pino
32
199
Torre Guardia
C.to Vivo
496
Grotte del Pisco
Marmolata
P. di Tèrito

Cala del Tombosiello
Belv.re di Migliara
202
Gr.ta Vela
Gr.ta dei Santi
Gr.ta Rossa
Cala Ventroso

Cala del Limmo
59
Gr.te di Stallàttiti
P. Orticella
Grotticella d' Insuro
Gr.ta Verde
103

M. Forte
105
Cala Spravata
P. Marmolata
P. del Tuono
Cala S. Costanzo
P. Ventroso

Capo Ruglio
Scalo di Limmo
30
P. dell' Articola
Sc.o Marcellino

P. Carena
41
Faro

TIRRE E

6

ISOLA DI CAPRI

MARINA GRANDE

Situated on the Northern coast at the point in which the island narrows into its characteristic "bottleneck", Marina Grande is the main port of Capri, the mooring place for ferries from Naples and Sorrento and the tourist boats that take visitors to Grotta Azzurra or around the island. The port was built in 1928 under the shelter of a long wharf and occupies a section of the beach (a free part and a part occupied by bathing establishments) which runs along the entire inlet in which the town has developed. It is the island's third biggest town, in size and number of inhabitants, after Capri and Anacapri and, due to its excellent facilities, it is much frequented by tourists particularly during the summer and is the classical departure point for trips and visits to the various points of naturalistic and cultural interest on the island. In the immediate vicinity of Marina Grande stands the little that remains of Emperor Augustus' Seaside Palace and, down below, the majestic ruins of Tiberius' Baths (belonging to Augustus' villa).The archaeological area can be reached on foot by following a short path (via the Seaside Palace) along which

Views from Marina Grande and the port

9

you come across some beautiful villas containing valuable items from the Seaside Palace excavations. Near the port, in Piazza della Vittoria, there is the bottom station of the funicular railway which takes the shortest route to the panoramic terrace of the town of Capri. You can walk up the same way to enjoy wonderful views and the panorama of the island offered by the various roads that climb up through the vegetation to the town. Going up via Colombo you enter, after a short while, via Marina Grande, lined by villas, gardens and hotels, some of which stand on archaeological sites where important Roman ruins have been discovered (a sarcophagus, a marble altar and some small statues). Almost immediately afterwards, you come to the start of the Phoenician Steps, which lead all the way up to Anacapri. Extremely close by stands the church of St. Constant or "Madonna della Libera" built on the site of ruins from Roman times, around the 8th century. Modified during the 10th and 11th centuries and then, by order of Count Giacomo Arcucci, in the 14th century. It conserves in its interior, four columns and some precious marble works coming from one of the imperial villas on the island. Dedicated in ancient times to the patron saint of Capri (the patriarch of

10

Picturesque corners of Marina Grande, the port and Monte Solaro

Constantinople, St. Constant), it is visited every year, on 14th May, by a solemn procession of fishermen who carry here, from the church of St. Stephen in Capri, the silver bust of the saint, which is taken back to Capri a few days later. Continuing further on, the road offers breathtaking views of Marina Grande, Capri and the road that leads from Capri to Anacapri; in the vicinity of the top station of the funicular railway, you pass beside the two cemeteries of Capri, the Catholic cemetery (1875) and, in the thick vegetation, the non-Catholic cemetery, set up in 1878 by the Capri doctor Ignazio Cerio to ensure a worthy burial for those who did not follow the religion of the Roman Catholic Church. As an alternative to this route, you can take the panoramic road of St. Francis, which bears this name due to the presence in the vicinity of a small fort built at the start of the 19th century by the French on the site of a pre-existent monastery dedicated to the saint. The road, which leads up steps to the Piazzetta (Piazza Umberto I) of Capri, is entered having gone all the way along via Ruocco from the port. A last alternative for reaching Capri, a shorter but steeper route, is via Truglio which follows the path of the funicular railway for a while and climbs up to meet via Acquaviva, which leads into the Piazzetta. In the area around via Truglio remarkable finds from imperial times have been brought to light, the most outstanding of which is a statue of Tiberius currently exhibited at the Louvre.

1) Sunset on Marina Grande

2) Aerial view

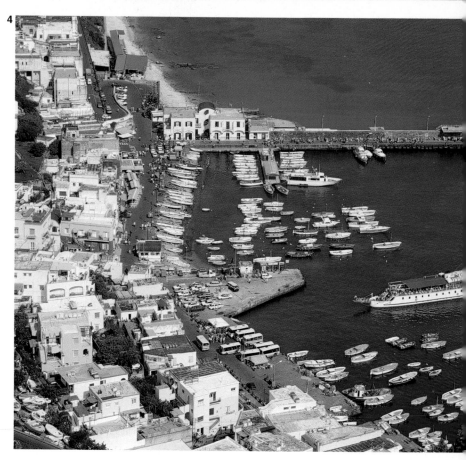

1) Church of San Costanzo
2-3-4-5) Views of the port of Marina
   Grande seen from above

Photo on pages 16-17:
Marina Grande by night

This is the name given to the ruins of what must have been the bathing area of Augustus' grand villa. Studies conducted on the ruins suggest that the complex, built in Augustus' time and probably modernized or expanded during the rule of his successor Tiberius, consisted of impressive walls built in *"opus reticulatum"* terminating in an exedra-nymphaeum, with walls completely covered with precious marble, adorned with a colonnade and linked to the beach by a flight of steps, a small port and tanks used for breeding fish and shellfish. Of the original installation, up to the present day there remain traces of the exedra and great walls, the landingplace and the swimming pools, in addition to many finds which were fortunately left behind by Hadrawa and are currently exhibited in museums. Depending on the fish bred, some of these tanks contained salt water, while others were supplied with fresh water from a special aqueduct. To change the water and ensure that it was always clean, all tanks were directly connected to the sea by a complex pipe system.

The imposing ruins of the Tiberian Baths

THE FUNICULAR RAILWAY

Built in 1907, it sets off from Marina Grande and, in five minutes, covers a distance of about 650 m permitting passengers to enjoy some spectacular views of the island, to the famous Piazzetta (Piazza Umberto I). At its point of arrival (138 m above sea level) opens out the terrace of the funicular railway, which the writer Alberto Savinio defined "[...] the ante-room of Capri, [...], a sampling room open to the four winds, providing a small but sure sample of all the delights offered by the island of goats." In fact, the terrace dominates the Gulf of Naples (on a clear day you can also see Ischia, Procida and Vivara), Marina Grande, the foot of Monte Solaro (the island's highest peak, at 589 m) and the surrounding panorama scattered with villas, orchards and gardens. The houses that stand to the east of the terrace have covered, over the years, what remained of the ancient Greek and Medieval walls, today almost completely hidden.

1

1) The cable car arrives at Capri
2) The *Loggetta*, observation point
3) Characteristic view
4) A lovely image of the cable car

2

3

4

LA PIAZZETTA

 Piazza Umberto I, as it is referred to officially, is exactly what the islanders and tourists call it: a "piazzetta" (small square). It is the heart of the town and can be reached from the terrace of the funicular railway or by passing through its ancient Medieval entrance. The square is delimited by the town hall, the steps that lead to the Church of St. Stephen and the impressive Clock Tower. On the façade of the town hall (the building dates back to the 14th century) there are two plaques in memory of Victor Emanuel II and Umbert I, while its internal courtyard houses some finds from Roman times discovered on the island. The Clock Tower is also known as the "campanile della Piazzetta" (the square's bell tower): in fact, while some believe that it is one of the many watch towers on the island, others believe that it is a modified version of the bell tower of the pre-existent church of St. Sophia, destroyed in the 17th century. But what makes this "Piazzetta" one of the most famous places on Capri is not so

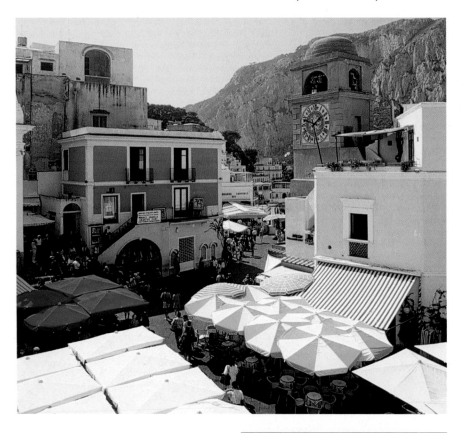

View of Piazza Umberto I, the famous *Piazzetta*

Photos on pages 24-25
1) **The clock tower, also known as the** *Piazzetta* **Bell Tower**
2-3) **Characteristic cafes and shops**
4) *Piazzetta* **observation point**
5) **Reproduction of the** *Piazzetta* **on the side of a taxi**

4

5

much these monuments, the façades of the characteristic architecture and small shops that surround it but the special mixed atmosphere of the worldly and everyday life that can be felt among the tables of the cafis, where you can meet tourists and artists, common people and the great names of show business and culture, all attracted by the simple, clean beauty of this small permanently crowded area. Until the second half of the Thirties, the few existing bars did not have tables outdoors: this novelty was introduced by the Gran Caffh Vuotto and it was from this moment on that the Piazzetta became "the" meeting place par excellence in the whole of Capri.

1) The bell tower
2) A fascinating nighttime view of the *Piazzetta*
3-4-5) Characteristic views

PALAZZO CERIO

The palace, which has rather a stern and massive appearance, is situated in the square of the same name opposite the church of St. Stephen. It owes its current name to the fact that it houses a Capri study centre named after the doctor Ignazio Cerio, father of the island's most famous scholars, Edwin. In reality, it was built in the 14th century by order of the Arcucci family, the noble and wealthy family of Giacomo Arcucci, founder of the Charterhouse of Capri and secretary of Queen Joan I of Anjou, who lived in the palace for a certain period of time. Modernized towards the end of the 17th century and expanded in the 19th century, it was also used over the years as an orphanage and as a hotel before housing the current institution.

1) The stairway and the entry to Palazzo Cerio

2) Characteristic street

THE CHURCH OF ST. STEPHEN

It is the island's largest church and was a cathedral until 1818, the year in which the diocese of Capri was incorporated in the Sorrento diocese. The building was designed by Francesco Antonio Picchietti and then built, probably on the site of the ancient church of St. Sophia, by Martial Desiderius from Amalfi during the last decade of the 17th century. The external architecture of the church, bright white with a baroque façade, is remarkable above all for the oriental motif created by the central dome and the vaults of the side chapels. Its interior with three aisles flanked by chapels, is enriched with marble taken from Roman buildings and interesting paintings. To the left of the presbytery stands the silver statue of St. Constant, the patriarch of Constantinople and the island's patron saint.

3) Statue of St. Constans   **4) The white façade of the Church of Santo Stefano**

1) View from the Church of Sant'Anna
2) View of the medieval town

3) Characteristic view
4) View of Via Vittorio Emanuele
5) Panorama

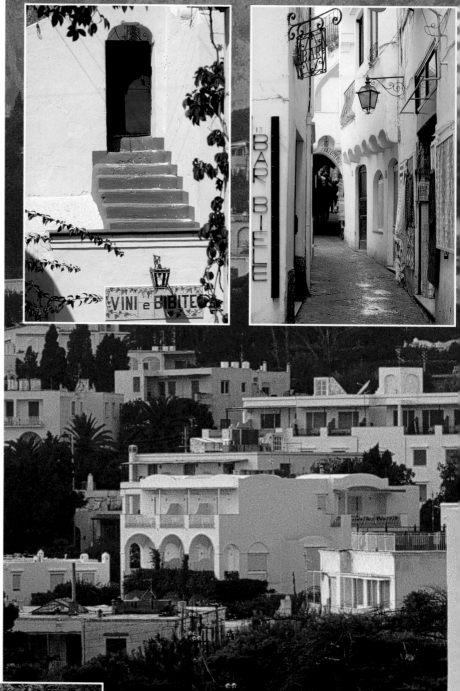

Characteristic views and typical Capri architecture

1-2-5) Corners of Capri
3) Via Camerelle
4) Via V. Emanuele and the Hotel
   Quisisana
6) Via Le Botteghe

Photos on pages 38-39: aerial view of
the San Giacomo Carthusian Monastery

3

4

CAPRI - REINA DE ROCA -
EN TU VESTIDO
DE COLOR AMARANTO Y AZUCENA
VIVÍ DESARROLLANDO
LA DICHA Y EL DOLOR LA VIÑA LLENA
DE RADIANTES RACIMOS
QUE CONQUISTÉ EN LA TIERRA
PABLO NERUDA

5

6

A remarkable example of Medieval architecture, the Charterhouse dedicated to the apostle James stands at a short distance from the centre of Capri in an area, in part, cultivated with olive trees and vine and, in part, occupied by recent buildings that create a certain contrast with its 14th century style. The construction of the great monastic complex, build by order of Count Giacomo Arcucci, the secretary and treasurer of Queen Joan I of Anjou, began around 1363 and was then resumed between 1371 and 1374. The early centuries of the monastery's history, like that of the whole island, were marked by the devastating raids by Ottoman pirates, like the raid of 1553 in which it was sacked and set on fire by the pirate Dragut or the one that took place eleven years later, which made the Carthusians decide to build a tower of defence on its Southern side, which collapsed in 1808. During the same year, Napoleon's government ordered the suppression of the Charterhouse, the annulment of its many privileges (which had, in some periods, been the cause of considerable protest by the island's population), the confiscation of all its assets and the expulsion of all the monks from the island. Having been used for housing the troops, in 1815 the complex was employed by the Bourbons as a prison and later as a home for veteran or invalid soldiers and, finally, from 1860 till the start of the 20th century, as a place of confinement for soldiers guilty of indiscipline or more serious offences. In the early years

The Great Cloister of the Carthusian Monastery

1

2

of the century, the Charterhouse risked passing into the hands of a company that intended to convert it into a hotel complex and escaped this fate as a result of the intervention of Benedetto Croce, being entrusted first to the Ministry of Education and later to the Ministry for Arts and Culture. In 1927 a restoration project was undertaken to return the ancient buildings to their splendour. Further work was carried out at the end of the Eighties. A visit to the Charterhouse enables you to observe, around the primitive Medieval complex, the outcome of the various restoration projects (the first was undertaken immediately after Dragut's raid in 1553), modifications and additions that succeeded one another over the centuries. Following the avenue leading to the monastery along which is situated the building once occupied by the monastery's chemists' laboratory and the Women's Chapel, you come to the church of St. James (beside the entrance to the Charterhouse). The ogival portal, the lunette of which is crowned by a 14th century fresco depicting the Virgin Mary and the Child between Saints Bruno and James, beside which appear Queen Joan I and Count Arcucci, gives access to its austere single-aisle interior (restored in 1927), with elegant cross vaults and 17th and 18th century frescos. From the tower that stands beside the church you enter the Charterhouse itself, part of which is occupied by the buildings dedicated to the monks' daily activities (the monks' cells, warehouses, stables and rooms for entertaining visitors and pilgrims who did not belong to the Carthusian order). The largest part is occupied by the convent of seclusion, formed by cloisters (the minor 14th century cloisters, modified during the following century and the major cloisters dating back to the end of the 16th century), the gallery, the refectory, the chapter-house, the fathers' cells, the prior's apartment and the Clock Tower (both of the

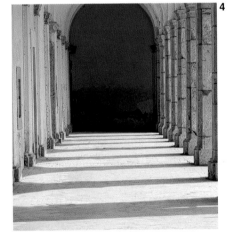

1) A characteristic detail of the Small Cloister of the Carthusian Monastery
2) The Great Cloister of the Carthusian Monastery
3) The majestic architectural complex of the Carthusian Monastery among olive trees and vineyards
4) Detail of the cloister

43

latter were added during the 17th century). The refectory area and the gallery area that was used for connecting the two cloisters has housed, since 1974, the museum dedicated to Karl Wilhelm Dieffenbach, which conserves numerous works (including some original views of Capri such as *"Marina Piccola" and "Le Grotte Marine" (the Seaside Caves)* by the controversial German painter who lived on Capri between the 19th and 20th centuries. In an adjacent room, you can admire valuable archaeological finds, an altar and two Roman marble statues brought to light in 1964 during research work carried out on the water in Grotta Azzurra: ruined to a considerable extent by the corrosive action of the water and salt, one represents a triton and the other the God Poseidon. The minor cloisters, enclosed by an elegant portico with 15th century round arches supported by pillars dating back to Roman times adorned with capitals, in part Roman and in part Byzantine, are contrasted by the adjacent Clock Tower in baroque style. Round arches, resting on larger pillars. They also frame the major cloisters on which the cells of the Carthusian fathers' cells overlooked: some of these now house the "Virgilio Marone" secondary school, the chapter-house and other rooms. Below the cloisters stands a large tank constituting the water supply for the complex which has a remarkable lunette vault. On the righthand side of the cloisters, added in the 17th century and not part of the classical design of Carthusian monasteries, is situated the prior's apartment and annexed garden, today a lookout from which you get a magnificent view of the sea, the Faraglioni and Punta Tragara.

1) The Great Cloister of the Carthusian Monastery
2) Statue of Triton recovered from the bottom of the Blue Grotto
3) Head of a Roman era statue discovered in the Blue Grotto
4) Panoramic view of the San Giacomo Carthusian Monastery

Interior of the Church of San Giacomo:
17th century frescoes

AUGUSTUS' GARDENS

The beautiful public gardens, situated at a point sheer above the sea at a short distance from the Charterhouse of St. James, were set up at the start of the century by Friedrich August Krupp, an extremely rich German industrialist who lived between the 19th and 20th centuries. The terraces, set in a luxuriant vegetation formed by various kinds of trees and brightly-coloured flowerbeds in bloom and adorned with beautiful statues (at the bottom of the area with the children's playground, there is also a stele by Giacomo Manzy dedicated to Lenin, who was on Capri at the start of the century), were constructed in the Thirties when, Mr. Krupp having died many years earlier, the gardens were expropriated from the Commune and opened to the public. From the park you get a spectacular view of the town of Capri, the Faraglioni and Marina Piccola. The park was named after Emperor Augustus in 1918 for "political" reasons: immediately after the first world war, the Commune felt that it was better to avoid using a German name like Krupp. Nicknamed the "King of cannons", Krupp lived in Capri from 1898 to 1902, the year in which he died in Germany, and played a leading role both in the determining the appearance of some places on Capri (he was responsible, not only for this park, but also for the construction of the spectacular street that bears his name) and in the island's worldly affairs at the centre of which Krupp remained for a long period due to fact that he was accused of being a homosexual and indulging in libertine behaviour. Irrespective of whether these accusations were true or false, the rich industrialist showed a growing love for the land that had given him hospitality, not only by embellishing it with the works mentioned previously, but also by making a significant contribution to research on the local marine fauna. He donated two boats that he had had built specially for this purpose.

1) The Stacks and Cannone observation point
2-3-4) The marvelous vegetation in the gardens of Augustus

Again it was Friedrich August Krupp behind the construction of this beautiful road that winds its way up, with its bold, spectacular bends dug into the rock sheer above the sea, fitting perfectly into the panorama and surrounding vegetation. The road, which is about 1350 m long, was designed by the engineer Emilio Mayer and built in 1901 on a large estate that Krupp had purchased in order to be able to construct a road that linked his villa to the nearby town of Capri. Now, via Krupp leads from Augustus' Gardens to Marina Piccola. Halfway along it there is a gateway, on the other side of which you come to Grotta di Fra' Felice, a cave that the German industrialist curiously decided to convert into a small residence on two floors to be used when meeting up with friends.

The spectacular Via Krupp

THE NATURAL ARCH

The large natural rock arch, situated near Grotta di Matermania, where it dominates the creek of the same name, rises impressively to a height of about 200 m above sea level. Framed by a thick, wild vegetation, it forms one of the island's most enchanting pictures, which can be admired from the two panoramic terraces. The imposing rock was part of the vault of a gigantic cave, originally underground which geological movements, erosion and the action of the elements, over the millenniums, caused to collapse almost completely, leaving only this part standing. The central opening of the arch is the result of the collapse of another piece of rock, which spared the two lateral pillars.

Lovely images of the Natural Arch seen from various perspectives

Photo on pages 54-55: view of Punta Tragara and the Stacks

GROTTA DI MATERMANIA

Situated about 180 m above sea level in the middle of a holm oak wood, this opening partially hidden by the thick vegetation can be reached by climbing up a steep flight of steps. The huge, semicircular cave (30 m long, 20 m wide and 10 m high) probably owes its name to the god of the land and fertility Cybele, in Latin "*Mater Magna*", to the worship of whom it was perhaps consecrated. It is certain that, during Augustus' and Tiberius' times, it was used as a large nymphaeum, as is witnessed by the Roman coating that can be seen on the walls. According to the research work carried out, archaeologists believe that inside the cave, in addition to some secondary rooms, the Romans had built a large hall with a reinforced vaulted ceiling to prevent the risk of collapse and a levelled floor to counteract the natural sloping of the ground. It was all coated with marble and mosaics (part of which were in all likelihood removed between the end of the 18th century and the 19th century, during Ferdinand IV's reign) and fitted out with seats and couches for those present to relax on.

Images of the Matermania Grotto

MARINA PICCOLA

The well-equipped tourist resort, which stretches along the southern coast of the island opposite Marina Grande, lies in an inlet on the slopes of Monte Solaro. From Capri you can reach it on foot starting from the Piazzetta first along via Roma and then via Marina Piccola. At a short distance from the cross-roads with the road that leads to Anacapri, in the vicinity of which stands the picturesque "Casa del Solitario", built into the rock of Monte Solaro open the caves including Grotta dell'Arco and Grotta delle Felci, in which prehistoric finds have been brought to light. There follows a section, flanked by some beautiful private villas and gardens, which offers splendid views of the Faraglioni, Punta Tragara and the town of Marina Piccola. Going down towards the village, the road meets via Krupp and ends at the square in front of the small church of St. Andrew, built at the start of the century and restored at the end of the second world war to repair the serious damage caused by the explosion of a mine. Further on you come to the "Scoglio delle Sirene" (Mermaid's Rock), which has a small wharf and divides the inlet of Marina Piccola into two bays (Marina di Pennauto and Marina di Mulo) occupied by bathing establishments. If you take via Krupp, you come to the rocky beach of Torre Saracena, whose name calls to mind the raids by pirates who spread terror on the island during the 16th century.

Marina Piccola and the Stacks

1) Marina Piccola
2) Swimming resorts on Marina Piccola
3-4) The Stacks

4

2

4

5

3

1) Panorama
2) Marina Piccola
3) Marina Piccola seen from the sea
4) Marina Piccola: the church of S. Andrea
5) Marina Piccola and the Stacks

1

It was defined the "sad, harsh and severe house", "a house like me", by Curzio Malaparte, the great Italian writer who had it built on Punta Massullo at a point which would be somewhat of an understatement to define panoramic due to its indescribable beauty. The residence, built between 1938 and 1949 on a design by Adalberto Libera (the designer of the Congress Palace of Eur in Rome), stands out clearly, due to its original architecture, from the constructions typical of the island. Surrounded by a pinewood, it has a two-floor structure painted red, stretching out towards the sea and interrupted only by the scenic steps that lead up to the solarium, a flat surface defined by a slight curve of white brick arranged in an arc, like a sail: some art critics have interpreted these features as a enchanting reference to the sacrificial altars of the ancient temples. The interiors, to which Curzio Malaparte made considerable changes with respect to Libera's design, are both simple and stylish at the same time. In the drawing-room, the writer had a large closed fireplace built, not set into a wall but into a large sheet of crystal from you can see the fire's flames, as if in a picture, with the Faraglioni and the Rock of Monacone in the background.

The extraordinary villa of Curzio Malaparte at the tip of Punta Massullo

THE FARAGLIONI

The three famous gigantic rocks emerging from the water owe their characteristic form to the corrosion of the waters and action of the rain and wind. The first, known as "Faraglione Stella" or "Faraglioni di Terra" (111 m high), is joined to the island by a strip of land. On the second, the "Faraglione di Mezzo" (81 m high), there is the "subway", a remarkably large natural arch through which you can transit in a boat. The third Faraglione, known as the "Faraglione di Fuori" or "Faraglione Scopolo" (105 m high), is separated from the previous one by a narrow (8 m) stretch of sea and is the home of a special kind of lizard (blue lizard of the Faraglioni), the same colour as the sky and the sea.

Photos on pages 64-69: enchanting views of the Stacks.
On page 64, lower left, a view of the Monacone cliffs

VILLA JOVIS

Built at the top of Mount Tiberius (334 m), the most impressive of the Roman villas on the island of Capri covers a surface area of over 6000 m². It was built by order of Emperor Tiberius, even though some slightly earlier finds brought to light during archaeological excavations in the area around the tanks suggested that Augustus had identified in that area an ideal place for building a residence. All in communication with one another by an intricate group of corridors, steps and passages, the various rooms of the villa, which probably occupied four floors on one side and two on the opposite side, were organized around an enormous rectangular area used for collecting rain water which, in turn, covered a tank with an extremely large capacity (in part built into the rock and in part made of brick) divided into several rooms designed for the same purpose. The imperial apartments, separated from the rest of the building and the magnificent loggia (over 90 m long) sheer above the sea and overlooking a splendid panorama, were situated on the North side, that is, in the area in which the view of the Gulf of Naples was more spectacular. On the opposite side, to the South, there was the spa area. On the East side, towards the Gulf of Salerno, there was the semicircular hall of the guest quarters, with the various rooms for representation and the imperial chancellery, while on the West side were situated the kitchens and service rooms, such as warehouses and storehouses. To the South, at some distance from the ruins of the villa are those of the "Lighthouse Tower", along the outside of which runs a flight of steps that climbed up in a spiral around the walls. Despite its name, the construction was probably not used as a lighthouse for ships sailing off the island but, apparently, as a signalling tower used for communicating with other centres equipped with similar buildings. According to the tale, Tiberius even managed to communicate with Rome by means of a sort

1) Remains of the magnificent villa
2-3) Two views of the villa
4) Plan of Villa Jovis

4

**Villa Jovis: views of the western area
and the kitchen quarters**

of "tam tam" based on smoke and fire signals, and to receive messages from the capital thanks to this tower, which thus enabled him to fulfil his imperial functions without leaving the island. The Roman historian Suetonius writes that, almost as a premonition, the tower collapsed as a result of an earthquake a few days before the emperor died. At a short distance from the lighthouse-tower you can see a precipice which, according to a tradition with no historical foundation was "Tiberius' leap", that is, the place off which the emperor made condemned men throw themselves. To the northeast, near the guest quarters, stands, on the villa ruins, the small church of St. Maria del Soccorso, which is even today a place of pilgrim for the island's fishermen who venerated the local Madonna. As early as the start of the 18th century, research work was carried out on the villa by order of the King of Naples, Charles III, aimed, as was often the case during this period, not at preserving but removing the marble, mosaics, wall decorations, furniture and valuables for transportation elsewhere or reuse as materials for other works. The same can be said, even more so, for the excavations carried out between the 18th and 19th centuries during Ferdinand IV's reign by Norbert Hadrawa who, here as elsewhere on the island, did not hesitate to strip the ruins of what he judged to be of value or worthy of interest. Further research work was carried out with a more scientific intention in 1827. Examples of the material removed during the course of these excavations which can be admired are a Roman floor rebuilt at the Royal Palace of Capodimonte, other marble floor decorations in the church of St. Stephen, two marble puteals decorated in relief and one marble relief kept at the National Museum of Naples. The ruins, despite the fact that they were entrusted to the father of the church of St. Maria del Soccorso, were subsequently, in part, abandoned and overgrown by the vegetation and, in part, occupied by local shepherds and farmers with their activities. In 1932, a further campaign of excavations was finally organized, thanks to which the ruins were freed not only of their abusive occupants but also of the waste material that had accumulated there over the centuries and that, once removed, confirmed the "cultural sacking" of a large part of the embellishing works and even of part of the villa's structure. The archaeological area was inaugurated in 1937 on the two thousandth anniversary of Augustus' birth, as is indicated on a memorial tablet. Unfortunately, the ruins are currently in part covered by overgrown vegetation again and new work is necessary.

Views of Marina Grande seen from Villa Jovis

Remains of Villa Jovis and the Soccorso Church

Surrounded by olive groves and vineyards, Anacapri, the second largest town on the island, is a tranquil tourist resort crossed by pleasant streets which reach the historical centre (Le Boffe, Caprile) and invite the visitor to discover its many beauties. The area was certainly inhabited in Roman times, as is witnessed by the many finds. During the Middle Ages, it was attacked several times by Turkish pirates but grew under the influence of the monks of the Charterhouse of St. James and Capri, from which it did not become independent until 1496. In the 19th century and the first half of the 20th century, it welcomed numerous artists and intellectuals (both Italian and foreign) attracted, like the Queen of Sweden by the poetry and beauty of the place. Associated with the name of the Swedish doctor and writer Axel Munthe, who had Villa St. Michael built there, the town possesses many churches (of particular interest are those of St. Michael, St. Sophia and St. Maria of Constantinople) which fit perfectly into a quiet setting of pretty, low white houses. Totally out of

The Anacapri chair lift to Monte Solaro, and picturesque corners of the island

Anacapri

Sì, canterò di te, verde Anacapri;
dirò di quel silenzio che ti chiude
come una veste; canterò la pace
che in te fluisce, come fosse un sangue
dolce e benigno, senza turbamento.
Dirò della ginestra che incorona
la montagna, dell'elce e del carrubo
che hanno sì grata l'ombra nel meriggio;
dirò del fico d'india, che le palme
aperte offre alle stimmate del sole.

Ma ora è tardi: già declina il giorno
e l'ombre fanno azzurra la montagna.
Senti quel lieve pigolio d'uccelli,
quello sfrascare basso tra i cespugli?
S'è fatto tardi ormai: bisogna andare.
Ecco già su Tiberio un po' di luna,
una virgola appena; è luna nuova.
Un'altra volta... Or io discenderò
per quella via tra la montagna e il mare
e una lucciola avrò per compagnia
                    Alma Siracusa Vuotto

line with the dominant architectural style is the Red House, in the ancient town centre, an extremely elaborate tower built at the start of the century by order of an eccentric American colonel around the ruins of an ancient 16th century tower where the people of Anacapri were said to have locked up their womenfolk during the periods in which the men were forced to leave the village to work.

1) Façade of the church of Santa Maria di Costantinopoli
2) Characteristic majolica painting
3) Europa Palace Hotel: the only hotel that offers rooms with private swimming pools, a convention center and an attached health center, the Capri Beauty Farm
4) Gardens on Piazza Vittoria

Piazza Vittoria and panorama seen from Anacapri, with the statue of Augustus Caesar

Photos on pages 84-85:
1) Piazza Vittoria, Via G. Orlandi and war memorials
2) The Casa Rossa, an Aragonese tower from the 16th century
3) The Chapel of Sant'Antonio

3

The villa was founded by Axel Munthe (Oskershamn 1857 - Stockholm 1949), a Swedish doctor, philanthropist, writer and great lover of antiques. Enchanted by the beauty of the island of Capri on his first visit in 1876, he lived there for many years and around 1910 he was struck by a serious eye illness which forced him to retire to the Tower of Materita (which he owned together with the area on which the Castle of Barbarossa stands, Tower of Damecuta, the Watch-Tower and many areas of land), where the light was less intense than in Villa San Michele, to write his most famous literary work, "The History of St. Michael", published in London in 1929. Despite the fact that it is a literary and, in part, fictitious work, in which he inserted episodes or details about the villa that have little or nothing to do with its real history, the "History of St. Michael" is extremely useful for understanding Munthe's desire to create a residence in which he could surround himself with the ancient objects that he loved so, recreating an area that resembled, as much as possible, the style and refinement of the ancient imperial villas on the island.

1) The principal facade of Villa San Michele
2) Detail of Villa San Michele with the Sphinx
3) A portrait of Axel Munthe

AXEL MUNTHE
1857 - 1949

1

2

3

1) View from Villa San Michele
2) Phoenician stairway
3) View from the arbor
4) The kitchen
5) Villa San Michele: view

4

5

In the immediate vicinity of Anacapri, Munthe purchased, from a carpenter by the name of Vincenzo, an area of land used for growing vine where the only buildings were a modest country house and the ruins of the chapel of St. Michael: subsequent research showed that there was, in ancient times, on the site, one of the twelve villas that Emperor Tiberius had built on Capri. In this area, starting from 1896, he then began to built the splendid residence that can still be admired today, remarkable as much for its wonderful position and highly original architecture as for the number of ancient finds kept there within, a large part of which does not, however, come from excavations carried out on the island of Capri. At the entrance to the villa, there is a simple wooden portal surrounded by a marble frieze with animal and vegetable motifs, which leads into the entrance hall, adorned with a remarkable Roman tombstone and a mosaic floor with a design found at Pompei (Cave canem). Another Pompeian mosaic floor ("Death and the Wine") can be admired in the dining-room, furnished in Renaissance style. At the centre of the building there is an open-air hall, based on a large-space design with the tanks for collecting rain water around which the imperial villas were organized. Right in the middle you can see a Roman puteal decorated with bas-reliefs; the walls are decorated with fragments of Roman terracotta and bronze heads. From this entrance hall climbs a flight of steps up to the loggia above, from which you enter the bedroom, which is also furnished in Italian Renaissance style and adorned with replicas of Pompeian bronzes and a magnificent bas-relief of the Roman imperial period. Of particular interest is Axel Munthe's study where, in addition to the Roman copy of Aphrodite's head, a young man's head of the 4th century BC and the majestic mosaic floor which probably came from one of the imperial villas on the island, there is a Medusa's head: in the History of Saint Michael, Munthe writes that it was found on the bottom of Tiberius' Baths after a vision he had had in a dream but, in part due to its incredible resemblance with three famous sculptures of Medusa kept at the Vatican, it seems more plausible that it was purchased from an antique dealer. The Loggia of Sculptures is, however, the biggest attraction with its numerous statues, mostly late replicas of ancient originals, Roman fragments and other valuable works: the most outstanding is the marble bust (original) portraying Emperor Tiberius (according to some, however, it portrays his nephew Germanicus). From the loggia you move on to the pergola of the villa, overlooking the garden, with a lookout from which you get a wonderful view of the inlet of Marina Grande and the Gulf of Naples. At the bottom of the steps that lead up to the chapel, you can admire the remains of a wall in "opus reticulatum" belonging to the imperial villa which stood on the site in ancient times and other Roman ruins (the ruins of a cubicle and a floor from imperial times). The chapel, probably built shortly before the year 1000, was converted by Munthe into a library and music hall: on the outside, the main wall is decorated with a splendid Roman tomb relief portraying a mother with her son, while inside there is a beautiful 14th century font. On the wall of the terrace that surrounds the chapel, Munthe set up an Egyptian sphinx which was, in all probability, but contrary to what the writer states in his literary work, a replica of an ancient sculpture. This part of the villa offers a splendid view of Castle of Barbarossa. Below the terrace you can see the terminal part of the Phoenician Steps which lead up from Marina Grande to Anacapri. Finally, from the chapel an avenue of cypresses (planted by the writer himself) leads back to the villa: at the end of the path you can admire Lucius Carcius' tomb, a Roman work dating back to the 1st century BC. Shortly before his death, Munthe donated the villa to the Swedish State and it now houses the St. Michael Foundation, which is dedicated to humanist studies and research in the field of classical culture in general.

1) Bust of Tiberius
2) Shot of the Loggia

3) View of the Loggia, with Hermes at rest in the foreground

Views of the Villa and its fabulous gardens

Photo on page 94: view from panoramic observation point of the Villa

THE CASTLE OF BARBAROSSA

It was built between the 10th and 11th centuries by the inhabitants of the area around the town of Anacapri as a fortification to defend the town against the Saracens' raids which, accompanied by sacking, destruction and robbery, were extremely frequent even on the island of Capri. In memory of that terrible period there remains the name of the bulwark, Khair-ad-din, admiral of the Turkish fleet nicknamed Barbarossa who, in 1535 won over the resistance of the islanders and destroyed it almost completely. From the ruins, which rise up on a large sheer area (once covered by a beautiful pine forest which has been struck several times by violent fires) that dominate the sea, you can clearly identify the two towers belonging to the stone outer walls and, at the centre of the complex, a small chapel with an apse and barrel vault flanked by a bell tower. The castle (which houses an institute for the study of ornithology) stands on an estate belonging to the Swedish Consulate, which organizes guided tours periodically both to the ruins and the surrounding area, of great naturalistic interest both for its fauna and flora.

The massive outer walls of Castle Barbarossa

Reaching an altitude of 589 m above sea level, the mountain, situated on the Western part of the island, is the highest peak on Capri. The summit, on which at the start of the century a large tourist complex (the "Sky's Song") was planned to be built but was never completed, can be reached from Anacapri by taking the chair lift (in about ten minutes) or on foot (about an hour and a half's walk) along a pleasant itinerary that winds along a path first through a wood of oaks and chestnuts and then is surrounded by a thick, low vegetation, offering marvellous panoramas. The bottom station is situated in the centre of Anacapri, at the end of Piazza della Vittoria, while the top station at an altitude of 586 m above sea level, is only three metres from the summit of Mount Solaro. The best view, magnificent and unforgettable, can be enjoyed from the summit of the mountain, where there are the ruins of a fortress built on the site of a pre-existent Medieval settlement by the English during the period of the war against the French (1806-08). From here you can admire not only the island, with the other lower peaks, white houses and villas scattered in the green countryside, the orchards, vineyards and olive groves, the coast modelled by the various headlands, the inlets and caves, the Faraglioni and rocks that emerge from the water, but also the Gulf of Sorrento and the Gulf of Naples, the peninsula of Sorrento, Ischia, Procida and even the Apennine peaks and, down below, the church of St. Maria Cetrella with its small hermitage.

Panorama with the Stacks and the Monacone Cliffs

Photos on pages 98-99: unforgettable images of the view from Monte Solaro

THE CHURCH OF ST. SOPHIA

Easily identified by its characteristic dome, the church stands in Piazza Materita, once known as the "stone square". The building, which was built, according to the tradition, in 1510, was actually constructed towards the end of the 16th century on the site of a pre-existent church of Medieval origin dedicated to St. Charles. The date of 1510 probably refers (as indicated by an inscription on the façade) to its foundation, which took place the year which saw the abandonment of the 16th century parish church of S. Maria a Li Curti (today S. Maria of Constantinople, in the village of Carena, a short distance from the town of Anacapri). The church took on a certain historical importance around 1680, when the sailors of Anacapri, following the example set by the fishermen of Capri, founded the Pawnshop of S.Maria del Buoncamino at S. Sofia. The church (which was not consecrated until 1790) underwent several modifications during the course of the 17th and 18th centuries, which were carried out in various different periods and under the direction of various architects and engineers and thus resulted in the creation of a building in which differing styles are placed side by side in a disorderly or, at best, non-uniform fashion: the three-aisle interior, for example, has a barrel vault over the central aisle while the lateral aisles have domical vaults. The white façade, consisting of three parts and soberly decorated with stucco work, was built, like the bell tower, in the second half of the 18th century.

The elegant façade of the Church of Santa Sofia and clock

The temple, a baroque building constructed between the 17th and 18th centuries, was added, in the 18th century, to the existing Teresian convent of St. Michael, founded by Sister Serafina di Dio (1621-99). At the time Prudence of Nicole,Antonio di Pisa, was, together with St. Constant, the leading religious figure in the island's history. Completed in 1719, the church of St. Michael stood alongside the existing church of St. Nicholas of which traces remain and completed the monastic nucleus planned by Sister Serafina. In 1808, with the advent of Napoleon's rule, the temple was closed: the Bourbons had it reopened but the church lived a troubled existence until almost the end of the century; it was even used as an ammunition depot and an orphanage before it was, in the end, sold to a Protestant German nobleman. The interior of the church, based on a central plan on which an octagonal dome was set, presents, in harmonious corners with apses, beautiful painted wooden altars, an impressive high altar made of marble decorated with hard stones and important canvases of the 17th and 18th centuries. The most remarkable work is the splendid majolica tile floor which stretches as far as the area delimited by the dome, laid in 1761 by a craftsman from Naples on commission by the Prince of St. Nicandro. It represents the expulsion of Adam and Eve from the Garden of Eden, inhabited by all kind of animals among which stands a unicorn at the centre of the composition.

The floor and its details in the church of San Michele. The precious majolica floor by Leonardo Chiaiese depicts Adam and Eve in the Garden of Eden

THE IMPERIAL VILLA OF DAMECUTA

Easily reached on foot from Anacapri (in about three quarters of an hour) along a pleasant itinerary through the vine and olive trees which offers splendid views of the island, the archaeological area of Villa of Damecuta is one of the most interesting in the whole of Capri. The results of the in-depth archaeological research work carried out between 1937 and 1948 did not succeed in determining whether the villa, which must have been one of the most magnificent of those built in the imperial period, was built during Augustus' or Tiberius' reign: the damage examined on the works brought to light has enabled it to be established that the villa was abandoned after the eruption of Vesuvius in 79 AD (over forty years after the death of Augustus' successor), which had sprinkled this part of the island with ash and lava. This abandonment was probably for ever and, for the luxurious residence, marked the start of a dark period which was to bring it to almost total destruction: on the one hand, it was used in part as material for constructing fortifications and means of defence both against pirate raids in the Middle Ages and in the period of war between the English (allies of the Bourbons) and the French, and on the other, it was sacked and devastated on more than one occasion. There are very few remains, not even enough to attempt to reconstruct what the original structure of the building was like. It can only therefore be supposed that Villa Damecuta, like all the other imperial residences on the island, was extremely large and divided into many rooms linked to one another and embellished with stylish decorative works (the remains of columns, marble statues and sections of wall constructed in *opus reticulatum* have been found, but there must also have been mosaic floors, wall paintings and other ornaments) and surrounded by gardens. Nearby, on the perimeter of the villa, there is a watch tower built in the 12th century; it was purchased by Axel Munthe, who donated it to the Italian State together with the entire villa area, which also belonged to him.

1) The gigantic Damecuta Tower
2) A Roman cistern
3) The "Opus Reticulatum" of the Villa Damecuta
4) Plan of Villa Damecuta
5) Remains of the imperial loggia of Villa Damecuta

THE BLUE GROTTO

It is certainly the most famous place on the island of Capri, the most spectacular and without doubt, at least during the tourist season, one of the most crowded. Its name and beauty are due to the intense blue colour of the crystal-clear water in this cave formed over the millenniums by the erosive action of the sea. The cave consists of several enclosures: the largest of these, known as the "Duomo Azzurro" (Blue Cathedral), which is accessed through a natural opening artificially widened in Roman times and around 1830, covers a surface area of about 70 m in length, 25 in width and 20-22 in depth: the height of the internal vault ranges from 7 to 14 m. From this main cavity lead many corridors and passages to other underground ravines. The fact that the water is blue (Sèvres blue, as the colour is known, due to its resemblance to the famous French pottery) depends on physical factors in that it only filters the blue component of light from the outside which enters the cave through an underwater opening situated directly below the entrance. Due to the same physical effect, any object immersed in the water (which only becomes blue when the sea is slightly rough) turns a silver colour. Research and studies conducted over the years have suggested that Grotta Azzurra was a Roman nymphaeum (that is, a place consecrated to the worship of nymphs), belonging perhaps to the Augustan villa called Gradola (from which the cave borrowed its name until the 1828 explorations, when it was renamed Grotta Azzurra), built on the embankment overlying the cave: evidence backing up this theory includes the numerous statues found in cave's water during the Sixties and more recently, probably fixed to the walls of the cave originally, and the internal landing-place which can be seen on the right-hand side of the entrance, a sort of artificial platform.

2

1) The charm and beauty of the extraordinary sea at the entry to the Blue Grotto
2) View of the Blue Grotto

Photos on pages 108-109: lights, colors and magic of the alluring Blue Grotto

1

THE BELVEDERE OF MIGLIARA

Situated at a height of 292 m above sea level, it is one of the most panoramic points in the whole of Capri. Starting from Anacapri, it can be reached from the small Piazza di Caprile along the pleasant Migliara road, which climbs gradually, offering splendid views of Anacapri and the open sea as far as the island of Ischia. Once the road, which winds its way along the path of a more ancient road, was completely immersed in the countryside and surrounded by vineyards, orchards and woods, while today, particularly in the initial part, you come across a large number of villas and houses. The belvedere opens at the start of the small peninsula that juts out to sea with Punta Carena, dominated by the lighthouse tower. The panorama over the area below and the sea is marvellous, and you get an even more breathtaking view from the left-hand side of the belvedere, towards Punta del Tuono: the view here starts from the beautiful Cala Marmolata and goes beyond Marina Piccola to Punta Tragara and the Faraglioni, sweeping across the entire southern shore of the island, with the white, sheer rock faces, sprayed with the green colour of the vegetation, the inlets and the ravines that decorate the coast like precious inlays and the unforgettable blue colour of the sea that laps the entire rugged shoreline.

The ancient fortification of the Migliara Observation Point and view of the Stacks

THE WATCH TOWER

The circular tower was built by order of the Spanish viceroys as a means of defence against attacks from the nearby Punta Carena. It stands at a height of about 300 metres above sea level at an extremely attractive point of the coast on the cliffs that dominate the Cala del Tombosiello and Cala del Limmo below, from which you get a wonderful panorama. After a period of abandonment, it was restored and converted into a private residence. From the Watch Tower, you can reach both Punta Carena and the Belvedere of Migliara by following a short and picturesque itinerary.

The Guard Tower on the majestic cliffs that dominate the sea and sunset

Starting from Marina Piccola and heading West you come to Grotta dell'Arco and Grotta delle Felci (in which Neolithic finds have been brought to light) and then, beyond Punta Mulo and Punta Ventroso, Grotta Verde (which takes its name from the emerald green colour of its water), the Grotta Rossa (named after the vegetation that grows on it) and Grotta Marmola. From Cala Marmolata open out the Grotta della Galleria, Grotta del Cannone (from the noise of the backwash), Grotta Brillante, Grotta dei Santi (with the characteristic rock formations that resemble figures praying) and Grotta Vela. You then continue on, beyond Punta del Tuono and Punta Carena, with its lighthouse, along the western, less rugged part of the coast (inland stand the Watch Tower and the towers of Materita and Damecuta) on which there are picturesque inlets (Limno, Tombosiello, di Mizzo and del Rio) interspersed with mini peninsulas and headlands. Having gone past Punta di Vetereto, you come to the small opening that leads into Grotta Azzurra, along the northern coast that rises up more and more steeply, and the ruins of Tiberius' Baths before reaching Marina Grande. Beyond the inlet are situated Grotta del Bue Marino and Grotta della Ricotta, followed by Punta del Cannone, beyond which the impressive rocky coast opens into Tiberius' Caves (in line with Tiberius' Leap), Grotta Bianca (with two stretches of fresh water inside, Grotta Meravigliosa (decorated with stalagmites) and Grotta dei Preti. Cala di Matermania, from which you can catch a glimpse of the Natural Arch, is followed by Punta Massullo (Casa Malaparte), the Rock of Monacone, Punta Tragara with the port of the same name and finally the Faraglioni. Before getting back to Marina Piccola, you pass the "Sailors' Hotel" with its blue-green water, the large Grotta della Certosa and, finally, Grotta dell'Arsenale, used as a nymphaeum in imperial times.

1) The Green Grotto
2) The sea around Marina Piccola
3) Inlet in Marina Piccola

2

3

1) A marvelous inlet
2) The White Grotto and the Marvelous Grotto
3) The Ricotta Cliffs
4) The *Sbruffo* ("The Spray")
5) Inlet in Marina Piccola

5

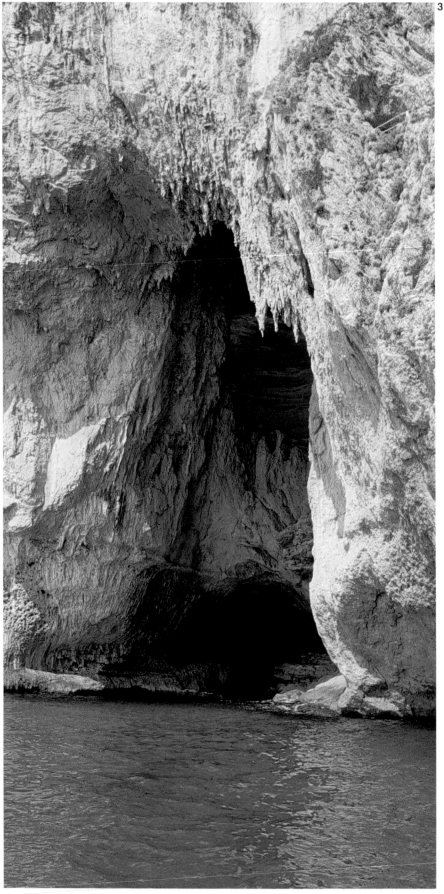

1-3-4) The Marvelous Grotto
2) The Small Natural Arch

1) Panorama of the coast as seen from
the sea
2) Sail Grotto
3) Coral Grotto

1-4-5) Views of the coast
2) Punta del Capo
3) The magical entry to Saints' Grotto

PUNTA CARENA

It is reached from Anacapri along a road bordered in its initial section by villas and characteristic Capri houses and, further on, immersed in a wilder panorama dominated by the colour of the rock and low vegetation typical of the island. The headland, which forms the tip of the small peninsula of Migliara, delimiting a sort of natural border between the western coast and the southern coast of Capri, projects a short distance from the belvedere of Migliara out to the open sea with its impressive cliffs that drop vertically forming huge rock steps and plunge into the water below. The flat end of the headland is dominated by the impressive lighthouse. Resting on a square white building, the white and red tower with an octagonal plan, still in operation today, was built at an extremely panoramic and clearly visible point, even from the open sea, in 1866. Over the years, Punta Carena, which represents an excellent point of observation over the surrounding area, was also employed for military purposes, as is witnessed by the constructions in the surrounding area: a fortress dating back to the early years of the 19th century, which was used by the French and English troops during the period of occupation, and a watchtower where the sentinels could shelter, built during the second world war. Moving on further west, you come to the bathing area known by the name "Bagni del Faro" (Lighthouse Baths), from which you can admire, towards the inland area, the Watch Tower, which rises up in a strategic position, dominating the Cala del Tombosiello.

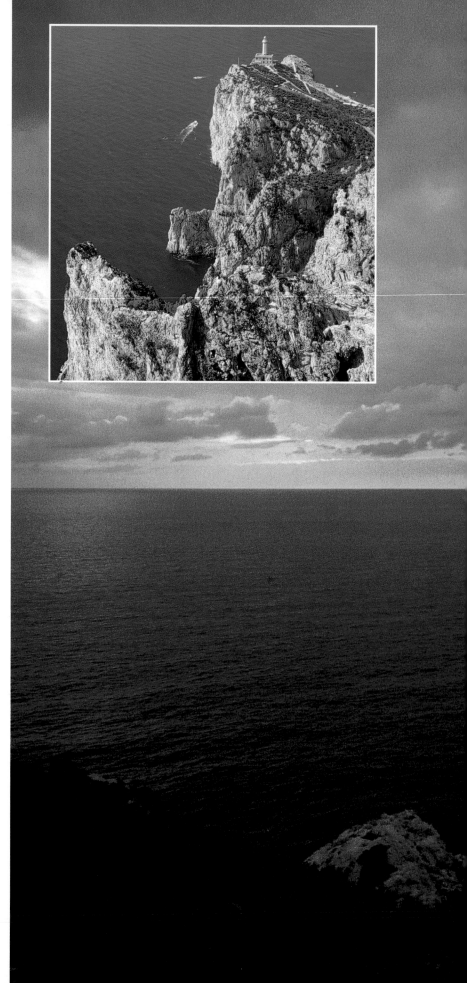

The precipice of Punta Carena and the Anacapri lighthouse